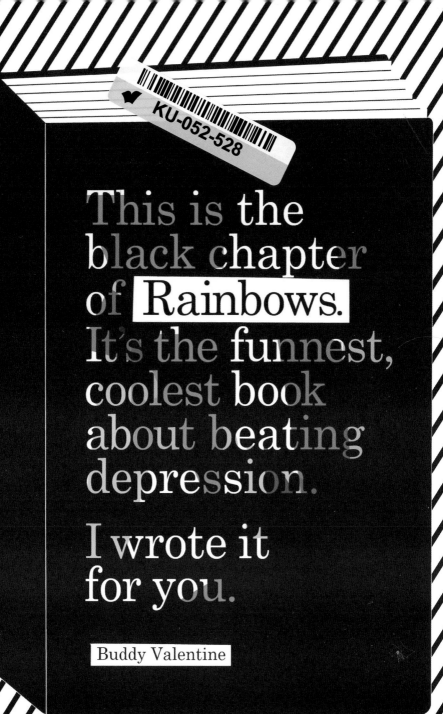

many/ many
thanks to you

Catalina Bae
Chris Baty
Chris Bick
Jacinta Bunnell
Suzanne Button
Kevin Carollo
Charlie Fuzzy Caterpillar
Four Winds
Lindsay Kaplan
Jamie Kennard
Tracy Kennard
Todd Kennedy
Lucy Legs
Tricia Mazzocca
Mom
Diana Mosbacher
Elijah Nella
Lisa Nolan
Sam Osterhout
Francis Parrilli
Mike Perry
Natalia Mehlman Petrzela
Micah Player
Annie Poon
Carla Rozman
Véronique Schwob
Carrie Schapker
Anne Sikora
Spruceton Inn
Debbie Urdang
Vern
James Wirth
Sebastian Zimmerman

for Penelope

T / A / B / L / E _ O / F _ C / O / N / T / E / N / T / S _

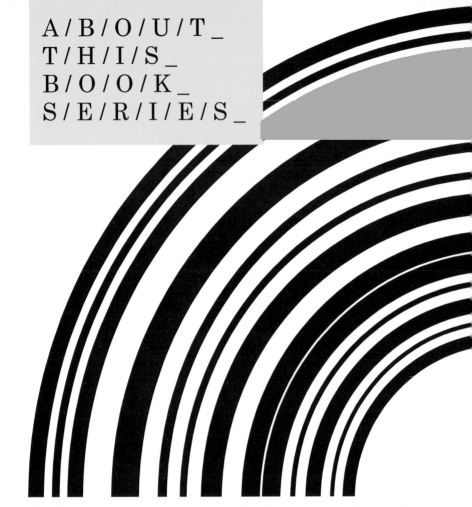

A / B / O / U / T _
T / H / I / S _
B / O / O / K _
S / E / R / I / E / S _

Real rainbows are not corny smiley faces on greeting cards_
They are badass muthafuckas and this book series is proof! It
was a secret before but now it/s amazing > Color/ in its endless
variation of shade and shape/ its brights and its darks/ its facts
and its mysteries/ is here for you/ always/ a reliable friend_

I am/ too_ My name is Buddy and I/m about to lead a tour of
over 100 mood–lifting/ mood–shifting ideas to help you better
enjoy life_ This is a let/s–repaint–everything look at managing
depression/ stress and anxiety/ full of ideas you haven/t yet
considered_ I won/t recommend something that I myself haven/t
tried and also I/ll snazz this up with personal stories/ rad art
and graphics/ activities/ interviews/ playlists and more_

While this book series is organized by color it/s not exactly color
therapy_ Rather I/ve used color thematically to organize mood

turnaround tips in small doses_ There will be ten booklets/ ten colors >> red / yellow / blue / brown / pink / orange / purple / green / black / white << I decided to publish the project one color at a time because nobody wants to listen to a friend go on and on with advice/ things to do_ You just get annoyed and then don/t do any of it_ Here you can start small_ I dare u to **TRY IT**>

Notice that silver is not on the list_ I love that color!! but want to mention that nothing in these books is a silver bullet_ < There are few suggestions anywhere that will make you feel 100% better immediately_ > Instead/ it/s the magic combination of small things – and I promise many suggestions will require as little as 30 seconds – plus your willingness to keep trying that will take you anywhere you dream_ Let/s begin_

I love you/
Buddy

B / L / A / C / K _

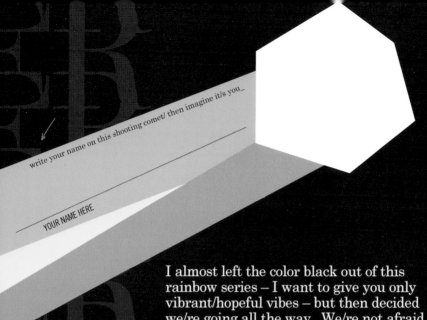

write your name on this shooting comet/ then imagine it/s you_

YOUR NAME HERE

I almost left the color black out of this rainbow series – I want to give you only vibrant/hopeful vibes – but then decided we/re going all the way_ We/re not afraid of the dark_ In fact/ let/s begin here_

Black tells many stories/ sad and otherwise/ but always its methods are definitive_ I think of the written word and its power of expression/ of novels that keep you awake/ magic marker protest signs demanding change/ secret messages that secure safety_

Here/s my secret message so listen up ☑ Although it feels like hard times will last forever/ they won/t_ They just won/t_ I/m going to say this again because it/s critical > When you are down/ you are certain you/ll never feel happiness again_ This is not true_ In fact/ it/s quite possible that a depressive episode – a period of despair/lethargy lasting more than a week and often endured for months – could lift almost mysteriously and without much effort_

That/s the good news – though I strongly advise against doing nothing – but there is some bad news also > Science asserts that once you have had a depressive episode your chances of another increase_ And if you/ve had several then the likelihood of a relapse approaches 100%_

9

But here/s the good news about the bad news > the more you can identify self–care activities that protect and improve your mood/ the better equipped you will be when miserable ghosts again knock on your door_

Did you notice something? When referring to those miserable ghosts on the doorstep I used the word *when* instead of *if_* I wish I could assert that once you/ve tackled the work in this book Sadness might leave you alone_ But it/s not that way_ Somewhere down the road Life has a black–ballooned surprise party in store for you/ no goodie bags_

But guess what? I/m a great event planner and my stepdad was a clown/ for real_ I/ve got party games like whoa_ Are you ready? My goal is to share with you some things you can keep in your back pocket to be ready for life/s quicksands and thorn bushes and banana peels_

I love that cartoony image > *Banana peels*! I don/t know why_ I just think it/s funny/ though if you/ve slipped on one/ you know it/s not funny one bit_ I want to tell you that I still slip on banana peels all the time_ I wrote these books about beating depression yet was often depressed as I wrote them_ That/s just how it goes_ The writing helped me/ though – I knew it would – So I kept going_ I/ll never stop_ You/ll find your own thing_ I hope this book helps_

I hate when people say stuff like/ ^The hard times make the good times sweeter_^ Whatever_ Or/ ^You/ll see/ everything is going to work out just fine_^ Or not_ I/m just gonna say/ ^Don/t give up_^ Remember that your Buddy has been there – so many of us have/ so many of us are there right now – but we got this on lock_ We/re leaving nobody behind_

Before we really begin pls flip towards the end cuz it/s so important > There/s a list of suicide prevention resources > websites/ hotlines/ even text support_ You are never alone and you always have options_ Go to page 55 of this chapter now so you know how to grab it should you or someone you know ever need it_ It repeats something I said here on this page/ something I hope you never forget_ >>>

R / E / A / D _

1 2 3 4 5

You don/t have
to read this cover
to cover because
the five pages you
catch might be all
you really need_

At a rather low time in my life I purchased a paperback book that billed itself as a sort of happiness how–to_ It had a yellow smiley face cookie on the cover/ definitely a draw_ I would read it on the subway going to my job and I/d practice some of its suggestions/ like forcing yourself to smile_

The book helped me a lot and not just the smiling_ It had insight/ thoughtful suggestions I felt encouraged to try/ and it inspired me/ so much so that I set it aside around chapter four_ Things were looking up_ I was practicing what I was learning and felt I did/t need it as much and that felt great_

I believe reading a book can be one of the most helpful things you can do to alleviate depression – that/s why I/m writing this one – but the truth is you don/t have to read the whole thing_ You don/t have to read it cover to cover because the five pages you catch might be all you really need_

TRY IT> The point is to try something_ Go to the library or book store and park in the self_help/wellness section for a half hour_ So often we feel alone but The Truth Is Out There_ Whatever/s on your mind/ go read something about it_ It/ll help_

There/s a funny story in this/ bringing us back to my smiley–faced paperback_ At the time that I was reading it I worked as a buyer for an online store that sold cute happy fun gift items_ So I proposed we sell this book_ It felt right_ It was cheerful/ fun and the bright cover read great online_

So we featured it on the site and it sold right away! Except our shipping manager brought the book to me before packing the first order_ "Are you aware that there is a chapter called Happy Sex?" Maybe I should have read the whole thing after all_ We didn/t want to get complaints from the moms of our young customers so sadly it was removed from the shop_ For years we had 24 copies of this book in a dusty box on a warehouse shelf_ I wonder what happened to them_

W / R / I / T / E _

You almost skipped this part_ You said to yourself > I/m not a writer I don/t like it I can/t write good_I agree w you_)I/m not a writer/ either_ Felt like a poser each time I said aloud that I was writing a book_ But u know what? Whether we believe it or not/ we/re both kinda genius at it_

Here/s how I know > Right now I see you grab a pen and a piece of scrap paper/ a torn notebook page or the back of a receipt_You sit at a desk a table on a train on a plane and look around and nobody/s there and no one will ever see this and you can even burn it once you/re done – your writing is that important – and then you just pour onto the page the contents of your mind_

TRY IT> Write+write and fast for 10 minutes like it/s a race – //don/t stop// – and don/t let your pen ever leave the paper_ Write through everything >> today things_ old things_ broken things_lost things_things wet + dragged through mud_ If you/re not sure where to begin/ try writing ^I HATE THIS^ over and over_ Something will come to you_

You don/t even have to read your writing once you/ve finished_ You don/t need to_It/s that good_ What makes it so is the fact that you discovered something maybe wrote + thought in a direction you hadn/t anticipate_ Your heart raced_ Your mind went weird places_ You left the hotel room trashed_

This is how I know your omfg poems or your smudged journal entries are gold on the page > It/s because they change things_ Your writing works better than a time machine_ It/s deeper than a mirror reflected upon itself_ It/s mightier than the sword_

Writing is a sabre and you < will > slay but don/t forget it/s also the butter knife you use on toast_ Take that glass–half–empty and smash it with your angry script or maybe head the opposite direction and fill it with comforting chocolate milk_ It/s up to you_The pen is a weapon_ It/s a tool_ It/s a paint brush_ It/s a spatula that flips banana pancakes_ It/s yours_

Your first written homework assignment is !! f r e e   w r i t i n g_ As described above/ just write and write and don/t punctuate and don/t stop and >> most important << *do not* edit // DO NOT EDIT_ I speedtype all my first drafts without even looking at the screen_ You can fix your jumbled punctuation later_ Or never_

14

TRY IT> Go for 10 min + 5 days in a row and see if it helps your mood_ Write about anything_ Write about everything_ //////// Try Natalie Goldberg/s *Writing Down the Bones: Freeing the Writer Within*/ an amazing+essential book that explores this powerful writing style via a mashup of inspiration/ memoir and zen_

TRY IT> Chris Baty/s *No Plot? No Problem! A Low-Stress/High–Velocity Guide to Writing a Novel in 30 Days* also rocks this same spirited/ judgement–free writing in a go–get–/em wild style_ It even comes with a free gift > a mad life–changing challenge that dares you to write a novel in a month_ You probably don/t need this level of commitment right now – with a measured daily quota of 1617 words to reach 50/000 in time – but you know yourself better than I do_ Maybe taking on something this big is *exactly* what you need_ < More from Chris Baty on page 18 >

Baty began National Novel Writing Month < NaNoWriMo > in November 1999 with a handful of friends_ Flash forward to 2017 and the cumulative number of November novelists this project has fostered boasts over 2 million served_ That/s a lot of talented co–workers to have on your team_ Should you accept the mission nanowrimo.org is gonna hook you up with a supportive structure and community you can lean on_ You need both right now_

TRY IT> Don/t wait until November/ though_ Baty/s book can help you make this very month your novelist debut_ Or consider a visit to a rustic outdoor [virtual] writing retreat at campnanowrimo.org that sponsors month–long groupwrites every April and July_ You determine the length and type of project you want to create but/ hullo/ you also get to literally [virtually] set up camp with other writers just like you_

This is critical_ When you are depressed/ the idea of being creative and being with others can feel impossible_ Somehow/ though/ when you/re on retreat in your [virtual] cabin in the dark and you/re typing away on your laptop with other campers and then you/re outside by the fire celebrating your accomplishments as you make yummy [virtual] smores/ well/ then the dark isn/t scary at all_

Let me rephrase that > The dark of depression *is* scary – I know this_ It/s like someone holding your head underwater – but I am trying to say encouraging things on the subject so you/ll take the chance & write about it_ I think it could help_

clarity that illuminates

reveals itself

abounds in the

now

TRY IT>

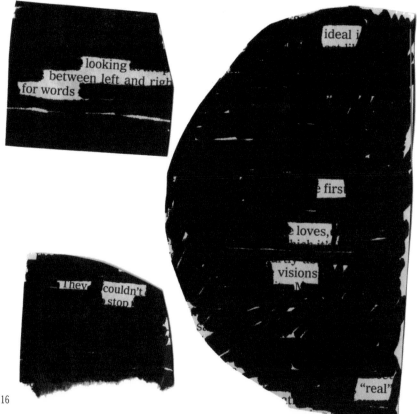

looking
between left and right
for words

ideal i

e firs

e loves,

visions

They couldn't
stop

"real"

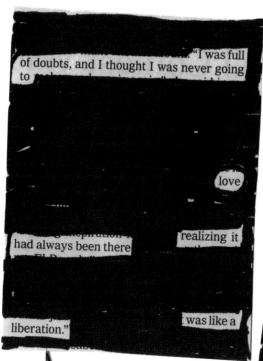

of doubts, and I thought I was never going to

"I was full

had always been there

realizing it

love

liberation."

was like a

"I said

I left

I'm going

'not so much

B / L / A / C / K –
O / U / T _
P / O / E / T / R / Y _

Even if you are not a poet < and you know it > there are all sorts of ways to write out heartbreak_ Try blackout poetry/ created by inking out existing texts to reveal new compositions_Take a scrap of newspaper and let a dark marker reveal the poem that lives between the words_ The poem was always there but *you* discovered it_

Chris Baty
nanowrimo.org →

DESCRIBE A DIFFICULT TIME IN YOUR LIFE AND HOW WRITING HELPED YOU THROUGH IT_

When I was in my early 30's, my life revolved around my work. And my work was not going well. I had founded a nonprofit called National Novel Writing Month and I loved it and it was growing like crazy. But I was still very new to running a business, and I made a series of overly optimistic, wildly dumb decisions that put the organization in financial straits.

Without a loan from somewhere, paychecks would be bouncing. The end of National Novel Writing Month seemed imminent.

This was a dismal time for me. I didn't feel like I could talk about it with anyone, and I was waking up in the middle of the night riddled with anxiety. I would spend hours lying in the dark, searching for a solution that didn't seem to be there. The worry bleached the color from my life, and I wandered through my days in a fog.

Out of desperation, I started a journal. I wrote about the bank meetings that didn't go well, the dead ends I was hitting with donors, and the hard conversations I was preparing to have with staff.

Curiously, I found that dwelling on my fears and playing out worst case scenarios in my journal always left me feeling better. Shaking the dark shards loose onto the page meant I didn't have to carry them in my head all the time. So I wrote a lot. I wrote in the morning and I wrote before I went to bed. Somewhere in all those words, I started to feel hopeful again.

We ended up getting the loan (hooray!), and, ten years later, the organization is still going strong. The whole episode taught me so many things, but one of the most important was how much weight a journal can bear. Writing may not change my life, but it always w

AMAZING! ☐ FAS TU

A/C/T/I/V/I/T/Y_

☐✓ BAD! ☐ BANANA

☐ DAZZLING! ☐ DEEP

☐ EXCITING! ☐ EXUBE

☐ FRESH! ☐ FU

☐ GORGEOUS! ☐ GREAT! ☐

☐ HOT! ☐ INSPIRII

☐ LOVELY! ☐ JOYOUS

☐ RAD! ☐ RADIA

☐ SPARKLING! ☐ SPECTACU
☐ SPLENDID!

☐ STUNNING! ☐ SU

☐ TERRIFIC! ☐ UNF

20

☐ WID! ☐ WINN N

My mom hates when cashiers say/ ^Have a good one!!^ because she thinks it/s weird_ That good ^one^ refers to *what* exactly?

I take issue with the dull/ overused adjective ^good^_ We can do better! Let/s embrace powerful/ wild words that gleam like geodes/ laser beams and fireworks_

TRY IT > I know you don/t feel so funny psyched extra–awesome magnificent life–changing and prismatic right now but your mission is to select a hype adjective on this page/ one you would normally never use/ and place it in a *spoken* sentence_ < Not email/ not FB/ etc_ but to an actual person_ > Do it today_

Before you say wtf/why? try it_ Force yourself to speak one single sentence in !!!/s_ Try this a few days in a row_

You know that feeling when someone near you uses a word you haven/t heard in a long time/ or ever? It/s **exciting_ What/s more/ the discovery is infectious as the word travels from one conversation to the next_

You have the power – even when ^crappy^ is the most accurate adjective describing your life – to bring a little zing! to those near you_ And that/ of course/ will come back around_

D / R / A / W _

I was naughty and I put
a bad word somewhere
on these two pages_
Can you find it?

Here/ take this imaginary pencil + grab this imaginary pen &
let/s talk about how drawing can improve your mood_ If you/re
about to say/ ^¡I can/t draw!^ this is for you_ I can/t draw/ either_

Let/s embrace the freewrite spirit of *No Plot? No Problem!* and
put that pencil/pen to paper and doodle scribble make mistakes
make something ugly embarrassingly bad/ laughable_ If it makes
you or someone else laugh then this scheme is already working_

TRY IT> Take something out of your refrigerator and draw it_
Sketch a glass of water/ then drink it_ Draw an object without
looking down at your page/ draw something with your eyes closed/
with your opposite hand_ Sketch a simple floorplan of a place_
Once/ friends and I attempted to draw the layout of a teen dance
club from back in the day_ Each version looked totally different_

Try making a map_ Draw what you see out the window_
Draw the contents of a cabinet or drawer_ When your
thoughts run in circles/draw something/ anything_
Drawing is a secret antidote_ My friend/ artist Annie Poon/
found herself stranded alone in a remote country house
in the woods and was terrified_ So/ room by room/ she
drew every single thing there was inside_

TRY IT> If you live in a larger city/ chances are there/s
a decent bar that hosts drink + draw events/ informal
meet–ups of all skill levels with live figure drawing and
good vibes_ You don/t have to be an art star to participate
and you might just make a friend_

Drawing is an amazing mindfulness tool_ You have to
focus > focus on something else/ focus on someone or
something right in front of you/ and go deep/ really see it/ really
discover it_ If you look closely at what you think you know –
really *look* – you/ll see things you/ve never seen before_

You don/t have to be able
to draw to be able to draw_
Sometimes I just write the
alphabet in odd ways_ Or I/ll
fixate on a word / a sentence
or something I overheard and
pen it into a loopy / bubbled /
lightning–bolted / cheeseburger
dream_ When my mind goes
round and round I/ll draw
tornados and hairdos_ Almost
without realizing/ I draw myself
advice/ if that makes sense_ I
might feel miserable but those
goofy faces cheer me up_

23

fifteen hangers (wood)

two saved cups

marshmallow drying rack

dresser

chinese statue

laundry basket

70's cat puzzle - has all pieces!

welcome g typewri

twin stools for a comfie tushie

chris

when Harry hit the Hamptons

tissue box

fake l

wrong time cuckoo

sneezy kitty pillow

oh no! two best friends have been separated. can you find and reunite them?

lamp with tacky shade

ordinary side table

the other velvet chair

cardboard elk head

skittle gree hoodie

goblets

loose drawer handle

breakfast nook

fancy pitcher

flowered jars

porcelain pitcher

rainbow adler-esque platter

mushrooms table cloth

acorn junk jar

paper towels

kitty box

pharmacy bottles

maira kalman picture

rubber green pot

nose rinse pot

hard-to-draw flower vase

stool & ladder

horse vase

mary had a little lamb sculpture

owl please acorn jar

r bottles

green marble table

coffee zizzer

stubby bottle

er oven

bent neck vase

mug

fridge

coffee Tin

in bottles

mysterious use vase

mug

old school p vase

gentlemens start your ovens Killer recipes For Guys by Tucker Shaw

missoni chair x 3

owl pitcher

Beach photo

mug

brain jello

Tea for

dinged-up dear statue

Be Wise Save Bank

24

silverware

mysterious black book

Yellowish seventies clock

ice cream lamps

teeny measures

utensils

blue willow tea cup

jelly bean side table

Ball

retro ... clock

wood grain coaster

two bowls

green apple

utensil jar

bed with lumberjack bedding

tote

shears

knife set with colored handles

designer matches

air freshener

architecture childrens book

dish rack

old sponge with green scrub layer

salvaged zip-lock

electric oven

silhouette

Maira Kalman print

hello hummel

guest roo

BIG WATER

rolled music chart

white fuzzy towel

adler ditty jar

scrubber on a rope

blue teapot

...d with ...t sheets

ballet dancer in blue tutu

ornately framed landscape of red flowers

mostly used toothpaste

the striped towel

toothbrush jar

spotless d...

2 french gnome lone smoking a pipe

cardstock sky-blue bird

flowers n mountains photo

keyholes dresser

mint green clock

red lips heart

dysfunctional burger timer

Confined to an empty country cottage during a week–long rainstorm/ the artist Annie Poon fought fear & loneliness by drawing every single thing in the house_ anniepoon.com

U.S.A. paint by number

Ballet in pin tutu

cleanser conditioner

...ee

two broken in tooth brushes

cool end

two paint by number

25

Art/illustration/design megatalent
Mike Perry – the supercrush behind
Broad City/s bouncy/trippy animated
sequences and rad ad/ventures for
Nike/ Coca-Cola/ Oreo/ GQ and more –
considers drawing a form of escapism_
^It/s about looking inside and trusting
yourself while not knowing where you
might end up_^ For more inspiration/
check out *Hand Job: A Catalog of Type*/
Perry/s curated compendium of 50
creatives who spellcheck hand–drawn
type in surprising ways_

mikeperrystudio.com

T / I / M / E _
T / R / A / V / E / L

You
can change
anything
in
less time
than it takes
to microwave
popcorn

—

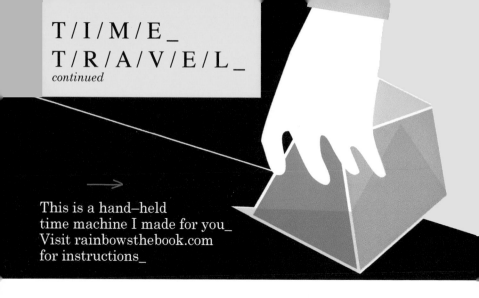

This is a hand–held
time machine I made for you_
Visit rainbowsthebook.com
for instructions_

When you are depressed it feels like time unravels/laughs at you_
You can/t imagine the future and the past reminds you with each
consideration that you were/are a fool_ The present suffocates
you_ You can/t feel/ don/t care + everything/s wrong gone lost_

Throughout this book series I/ll suggest activities small and
large that will help/ though at first they will seem impossible to
consider/ especially ^I dare u^ goofs like *Skydiving!* \ see BLUE
chapter_*Geocaching!* \ GREEN_ *Jazzercize!* \ PINK_ Know that
I know how ridiculous these ideas – even the simplest actions – feel
when you can barely get out of bed_

This is where time travel comes in_ Make time yours and commit
to doing your best for a mere 5 minutes_ Five minutes can change
everything_ Pretend you loove your job and are super outgoing for
5 minutes_ Give your maximum effort at the gym for 5 minutes_
Write in your journal for 5 minutes_

I began this experiment using a sleek black timer hung round my
neck – I had one from when I was a personal trainer for/ literally/
5 minutes – but of course the clock function on your phone is fine_

The timer setting – where you input your desired time at the front
end and watch it count down – likely seems most logical but I
prefer the stopwatch_ Having the numbers tick up rather than
down feels more optimistic_ See what works best for you_

Eventually/ if this method helps you/ see if moving your sprints
to 10 or 15 minutes feels right_ Go walk for 15/ clean your room

for 20/ work hard for 30_ Keep the minutes visible as you try your best at work/play/relaxation/etc_

I got >really< into using the stopwatch and began timing myself getting ready in the morning/ just to see how long it took_ That too helped my mood somehow_ Suddenly the start of the day had a new focus/ something else to think about besides d r e a d_ Then – is this odd? – it became a game > Can I beat yesterday/s personal best? I was training/ you might say/ and my efforts paid off_ Over time my morning routine grew faster_ I found shortcuts/ moved or combined tasks_ After a month or so I/d reduced my get–up–and–go in half_ Weird/ tiny victories like these gave me hope_

I/m not pushing time travel as like a bizzy productivity hack_ It/s just kinda fun and it/s helped me and it might help you_ I *am* gonna go a bit deeper into business$speak for a sec but we are only playing office and this is merely a game/ ok >>

TRY IT> Another time–bending tool I employ is a cloud–based accounting service known as FreshBooks_ < Try it free at freshbooks.com > While intended for small business time/money management/ I use it to push myself personally and creatively_ First/ I set up a pretend [company] _ < I wanted something exciting so mine is called Palm Springs Detective Agency_ > Next I made myself/ Buddy/ a [client] and created [projects] that correspond to things I want and don/t want to do_

For example/ whenever I think I don/t have time/don/t want to work on this book – even though it/s my favorite thing in life – I start the FreshBooks stopwatch on this particular [project] and it remains in the corner of my computer screen as I go_ Most often I aim for a mere 20 minutes of writing_ If it goes beyond that/ fun_ If I really only have 10 minutes available and that/s all I do today/ that/s awesome/ too_ It/s awesome because I did it_ I totally didn/t want to but I did it anyhow and that feels good_ Feels amazing/ even/ when you are depressed_ If you like/ at the end of your day/week/month you can review your timesheet and show yourself how/ despite everything/ you/ve logged some decent hours on behalf of your best client_ Maybe you/re not as immobilized as you thought_ In fact/ I think you deserve a raise_

All this measuring of daily life may sound technical or cold_ The magic of it/ however/ is that when you set out to tackle things you dread/fear – even for mere minutes – you discover you/ve made time your friend your travel companion your bitch_ Focusing on it will somehow help you forget about it entirely_

A / B / R / A / H / A / M _
L / I / N / C / O / L / N / S
P / O / C / K / E / T_
W / A / T / C / H _

The story of Abraham Lincoln/s pocket watch goes like this >
A watchman in Washington/ DC named Jonathan Dillon was
repairing the timepiece of our 16th president on April 12/ 1861
when news arrived of the bombardment of Fort Sumter/ known
as the beginning of the Civil War_

Dillon quickly opened the watch and hand–engraved a message
inside that read/ ^Jonathan Dillon April 13–1861 Fort Sumpter
was attacked by the rebels on the above date J Dillon April 13-1861
Washington thank God we have a government Jonth Dillon_^

So/ yeah/ maybe Dillon got the date wrong – we all do that – and
also misspelled the name of the fort_ And wrote his own name
three times/three ways_ But Jonathan/J/Jonth/ the only Union
sympathizer in his workplace/ intended the message as one of
support for the president at this historic moment_

It remained unseen for 148 years_

The discovery was made in 2009 when Douglas Stiles/ Dillon's
great great grandson/ pursuaded The Smithsonian to open their
archives and re–examine the timepiece_ Harry Rubenstein/
chief curator of *Abraham Lincoln: An Extraordinary Life* said/
^It/s sort of amazing/ when you think that two years before the
Emancipation Proclamation/ Abraham Lincoln is carrying this
hopeful message in his pocket, and never knowing it_^

On the previous page we talked about time in terms of stopwatches
and on–the–clocks and parcelled minutes_ Here I just want to
remind you that anything everything has a hidden story_ This
timepiece tale confirms that things are never what they seem_
There is hope all around you that you can/t yet see_

The reason I know this? It's because I've placed a secret message
inside this very pocket watch to the right_ Here/ it/s yours xx

A A A
B B B C C
D D E E E E
G G F F
H H H
J J
K K K L L M M N

giving you an é so
you can spell the
super–motivating
word ^Beyoncé^

TRY IT >

S / P / E / L / L _
I / T _ O / U / T _

One word can be powerful enough to keep you motivated_ Download this page at rainbowsthebook.com/ trim out some letters and spell something meaningful to you_ Hang a tiny banner in a visible spot – a mirror/ a doorknob/ a lamp – as a secret reminder of your superpowers_

B / L / A / C / K / L / I / G / H / T _

I think blacklight is so weird and cool and wanted to mention it
here as a metaphor/ a reminder that sometimes dark causes
bright_ Surviving the most difficult times in your life often brings
the richest results_ That likely won/t provide much comfort
now but imagine your deep/dark moods possess inner blacklight
power/ the ability to make neons laugh and whites strobe/ to
ignite glow sticks and hot pink nail polish and sparklers_

How do you apply this concept to everyday efforts to improve your
mood? See what happens if you brighten up some basics_

Color Run / Night
Sydney / Australia / Feb 2016
Todd Kennedy_

Test out a pair of neon socks_ Stargaze yourself to sleep with a glow–in–the–dark constellation on your ceiling_ Keep highlighters and bright post–its on your desk_ Add colored lights in the yard_ Let's lighten things up – I mean/ blacklighten things up_

TRY IT> Think big and rock an explosive Color Run near you_ (Visit thecolorrun.com) Perfect for first–timers/ these non–competitive runs boom with head–to–toe splashes of vibrant color/ music and community_ Nighttime runs even provide blacklight headlamps_ These unique runs are billed as The Happiest 5Ks on the Planet so that/s gotta mean something_

G / E / T _ A _
H / A / I / R / C / U / T _

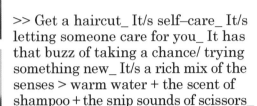

>> Get a haircut_ It/s self–care_ It/s letting someone care for you_ It has that buzz of taking a chance/ trying something new_ It/s a rich mix of the senses > warm water + the scent of shampoo + the snip sounds of scissors_

LAYERED BOB ⎯

It will make you more alert_ It will give you bounce_ It/ll make you more social_ > You/ll have to interact with your barber/stylist and other clients plus the folks that notice your cute new look_ This is good for you_

So many reasons to go get gorgeous but/ basically/ when you/re depressed your head carries so much hurt_ A trim lightens it up_

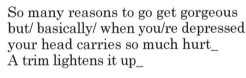

TRY IT > Leap into a big makeover/ a hair color switch–up or a bold change in length_ I dare u_< Is this tip on the superficial side? Yes!! Try it_ >

5–POINT ⎯⎯>

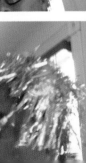

BOB+BANGS ⟶

PAGE BOY ⟶

PIXIE ⟶

a friend asked me/ What the hull does getting a haircut have to do with the color black?/ I placed this mood-improvement suggestion here because black is the most popular natural hair color in the world_

also ps >I know you were wondering > No/ this is not my real hair lol_

Writing doesn/t have to be an emotional outpour if that/s not for you_ A simple list can help your mood just as much_

TRY IT> One helpful list idea is developing a daily practice of writing five things / people / places / events / etc for which you are grateful_ Sounds corny / Sounds lame / I know / So what / Try it_ Use form on page 46 for a full week and see_

Studies assert that >> gratitude journals << lead to improved happiness/ productivity/ spirituality and more_ Even health benefits such as better sleep and stronger immune systems have been documented in people who engage in a regular gratitude practice_ The gratitude journal has staying power – backed by science! – and I highly recommend it_

It/s hard to be grateful but that/s the point_ Often the way out of this thing is to do the exact opposite of how you feel_ You/ll force yourself at first but soon you/ll realize that even on your worst days there/s that 1) nice cup of coffee 2) weather that can improve from one day to the next 3) the caring attention from your pet 4) maybe a friendly text_ There_ That/s five for today_ You can elaborate on those or not/ up to you/ but I suggest you be as specific as you can_ Being grateful in general is good but it/s more powerful to narrow in on the small things/ name names/ describe places/ etc_ Bring those five things to life_

Wait_ I forgot one/ srry_ There/s 5) reading this book/ knowing someone who wrote it was thinking of you and trying to help_ I wouldn/t blame you for thinking this exercise sounds like that sickly sweet // b e p o s i t i v e // but that/s not it at all_ I/m saying >> Be yourself_ Feel as you feel_ At the same time/ let/s review the day and see if there was anything good_

Now let/s discuss some list–making alternative medicines_ If gratitude feels to you like arranging flowers in a vase and you/d rather chase dragons then some of the following ideas – maybe more investigative or more critical? – might be for you_

this sucks	on a positive note
who am I to write this book?	I have personal experience
can I call myself a writer when I haven't written that much?	do u enjoy writing? yes_ hullo you are at a writers residency right now
not a doctor	i know i can help people_
how can i offer advice when i still get depressed sometimes?	to struggle myself keeps it real_ feeling good takes lifelong practice
i sleep all the time	i know i can do it
it's hard	it's fun

O / N _ A _ P / O / S / I / T / I / V / E _ N / O / T / E_

This isn/t me saying/ Be positive! This is me saying/ Complain all you want_ Get mad_ Be sad_ Be true_ Then/ just as an exercise/ no pressure/ look at the flipside_ Write it down_

TRY IT> When depressed try flip/reversing the classic pro/con or yes/no list so it reads con/pro or no/yes_ Why? Because this way you get to express how you truly feel <u>first_</u> That/s what/s so_ But then move to the right side and dig deep/ very deep_ There/s something hidden in the dirt right over there_ Look for it_ Consider the opposite of how you feel has minor? potential? in the Abstract? to be sorta? equally true_ The above no/yes is something I wrote when I was on a writer/s retreat for this book_ Immediately upon arrival I doubted myself_ Can I really do this? I wondered_ I decided I could_ This list helped me a lot_

Again/ do not think I/m here telling you to just b e p o s i t i v e – I know life sucks right now – but I/m asking you to practice/ even if forced/ the idea that there are bad situations and there are great opportunities and sometimes they/re one and the same_

Here/s a personal example > For years I/ve struggled with fatigue from my medications_ < I/ll talk about medication management in the BLUE chapter so more on that later_ > This means I fall asleep during the day/ every day_ The amount of time I actually have energy to work on this book is laughable_ But I/m trying anyhow_ Sometimes it feels great/ sometimes not_

My husband/ who I used to believe was the glass–half–empty type/ tried to encourage me in his own way_^Remember years ago when you were always getting sick and nauseous and sleeping for days?^ he asked_ ^Well // on a positive note // now you are just sleeping_ At least you don/t throw up as much_^

We both laughed_ Sometimes it feels the only true statement on the positive side is the reminder that at least things aren/t worse_ We also laughed because sometimes you just have to laugh_ < And laugh it off_ > You might find your truest pro / yes // on a positive note // could be merely something like ^Song I heard in grocery was good^_ Hey/ that/s great! You gotta start somewhere_ Good job_ Force yourself to fill in both sides of the list/ always_ Am trying to give you an option where u get to be grumpy but you gotta be grateful/ too_

Consider some other /note\worthy options >> Try a basic log like a sleep diary ~ sleep should be one of your **most** important considerations when it comes to mood management ~ and track when you get up and when you go to bed and how many times you wake in the night_ Prioritizing your schedule towards consistent sleep/wake times is important_ Use the log on page 49 < or download from rainbowsthebook.com> and see if it to helps_

Or a food tracker where you write down everything you eat and drink/ not with the goal of losing weight but merely to observe_ Why? Because the simple act of writing it down improves the area you are examining_ Keep notes of any purchase in a homemade expense log/ for example/ and you/ll find yourself saving money_

What if that logic carries over to a mood manager? Here you examine as objectively as you can your general daily mood_ Use a score card with a numeric range of 20 points > 1 being your highest ideal of life–changing happy and 20 as the worst level of upset/pain you have >ever< experienced in your life_ The range is slightly more expansive than your standard point system but that/s on purpose_ Mood is nuanced/ difficult to quantify with a mere number of stars_ < These forms and more pages 46–50_ >

Take a moment now to rate today so far on this 1–20 scale_ How does yesterday compare? You might be tempted to score it the same – especially if you are depressed – but use this system to take a closer look_ < Advanced > You could even split this into morning / noon / night_ Maybe you/ll notice the time of day you felt your worst and the one that felt the lightest_ If you had a better day/ or merely a less awful afternoon/ try to decipher why_ Was it better sleep? Did you exercise that day? What did you eat? Who did u see? Did you read or watch tv? If you can pinpoint the small things that improve your mood/ try to build more of them into your schedule_ Test if that can up your average_

Ok/ I know it/s not exactly that simple_ You can/t really measure some of those dark murky cold wet swamps your mind can lead you towards/ that/s true_ You know depression escapes logic_ You know the ghosts aren/t real yet you often feel trapped inside your own unrecognizable mind with ???/s that turn/turn_ Depression is a mystery/ a nightmare/ a horror film where it seems no one is getting out alive_

But *you* are_ You/re the smartest one in the movie_ Why? Because nobody can unravel this mystery better than you_ Slowly/ at your own pace/ become the detective_ Begin with gratitude or small lists_ Then maybe try a couple oddball things/ like reviewing a film or arm–wrestling the alphabet/ things to keep your mind busy_ < More found on pages 46–50_ > Keep going and you/ll see_ With notes in hand you/ll soon be cracking codes/ booking evidence/ kicking ass/ taking names_

While I/ve just hyped list–making know I don/t advise a ~~to-do list~~ for you just yet_ Stay away from lists that are super practical for now/ maybe not helpful_ Instead stick to exploratory missions/ investigative stories/ small steps to make your life better_

TRY IT> Consider the brilliant *Listography* series of list–making workbooks that will help you dream/ laugh/ remember and record your extraordinary life_ < More with creator Lisa Nolan on pg 44 >

HOW HAS LIST-MAKING HELPED YOU IN HARD TIMES?

Lisa Nolan
listography.com

▶ I started making lists when I was a young adult. I didn't realize it then but I was compensating for memory loss. I struggled with both anxiety and depression due to some trauma from my past and learned later that memory can affect people who have suffered abuse. Parts of my brain grew stronger, like empathy, reading people,fight or flight, but my memory abilities weakened.

I've also used lists in my life to help with low moments, to motivate for the future, and to maintain my gratitude for things. People often think of lists as boring old to-do lists or grocery lists. Not so! You can make lists about your life that can help to change or reimagine it.

List-making is meditative. You're reminded of things that you don't think of daily, and especially not when you're down, and that shifts your perspective. If I asked you to make a list right now of what you are most grateful for, or your favorite things to smell, or your happiest memories, it would actually change your brain chemistry.

I recently used lists to get me through a very difficult time, losing my father. My father was an angel to me. Watching him suffer and eventually pass threatened to destabilize the balance of happiness and sadness I keep watch on within myself. I wanted to stay present with what was happening and also present in my life. So I made lists.

I made lists on my favorite memories with my father. I made lists on things we said or did during our last couple months together, like watching *Good Times* reruns. I made lists on my worries, my fears, care-giving advice, and reminders. And after he passed I made lists about what I needed to do with his home and his things so I didn't remain stagnant. Last on my list was removing his house slippers from the place he last left them.

Lists helped me to get things done so I could move forward after his passing — exactly what he had asked me to do. Placing things in lists reassured me that they wouldn't be forgotten and gave me comfort.

The next set of lists I wrote after my father's passing were about my future, what countries I wanted to visit one day, and what I am thankful for. Lists to help me look forward.

My father would most likely say, "You've got only so many years... Enjoy them, Lisa. Be happy." And I'm listening to him.

A / C / T / I / V / I / T / Y _

a week of gratitude

thursday

monday

friday

tuesday

saturday

wednesday

sunday

A _ W / E / E / K _ O / F _ G / R / A / T / I / T / U / D / E _

Print this out and place it by your bed_ In the evening before sleep take a breath and look calmly at the day that has passed_ List five things / people / places / moments / etc for which you are grateful_ Even when things look impossible there is something_ Look for it_ For more about gratitude see page 40_

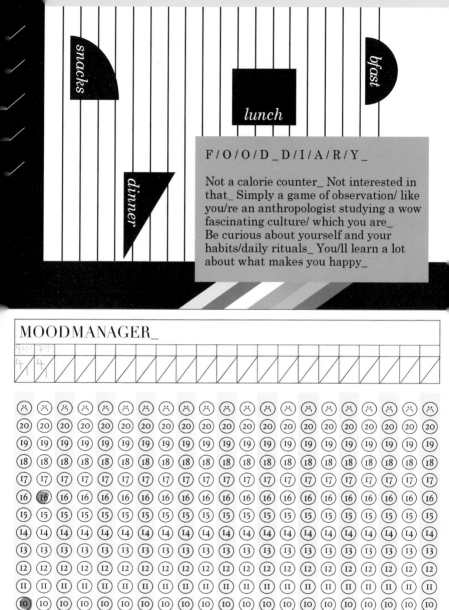

snacks

bfast

lunch

dinner

F / O / O / D _ D / I / A / R / Y _

Not a calorie counter_ Not interested in that_ Simply a game of observation/ like you/re an anthropologist studying a wow fascinating culture/ which you are_ Be curious about yourself and your habits/daily rituals_ You/ll learn a lot about what makes you happy_

MOODMANAGER_

9AM 7PM																					
4	4																				

M / O / O / D _ M / A / N / A / G / E / R _

No.2 pencil not required_ Use this simple form to examine your daily (even hourly) emotional state_ Sometimes it/s hard to know if things are improving because feelings can be squishy_ A study like this gathers more measurable data_ See page 42 for more information_

free downloads at rainbowsthebook.com

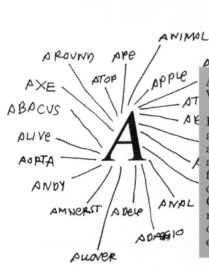

A / L / P / H / A _
V / I / L / L / E _

Easy as ABC > Grab a piece of paper/ select a letter of your choice and quickly write the first 20 words that come to mind_Why? Cuz it/s fun and random and a good distraction from less enjoyable thoughts_

at the movies

TITLE _____

OVERALL
☆☆☆

VIEW DATE ___ / ___ / ___

THEATRE _____

GUEST(S) _____

STARRING _____

M / O / V / I / E _
R / E / V / I / E / W / S _

Seeing a movie
= helpful for depression   ☆☆
= fun with friends   ☆☆
= great solo activity   ☆☆
= snacks   ☆☆

DIRECTION _____

ART DIRECTION _____   ☆☆☆☆☆

COSTUMES _____   ☆☆☆☆☆

SOUNDTRACK _____   ☆☆☆☆☆

DRAW A SCENE:

E / X / P / E / N / S / E _
L / O / G

Just for fun / no stress_
See how tiny changes in your daily spending can result in big $$_
Your mood is just the same_ Begin with small efforts and see how they add up_

=

FRI

SAT

THU

SUN

WED

draw
some_
thing

MON

TUE

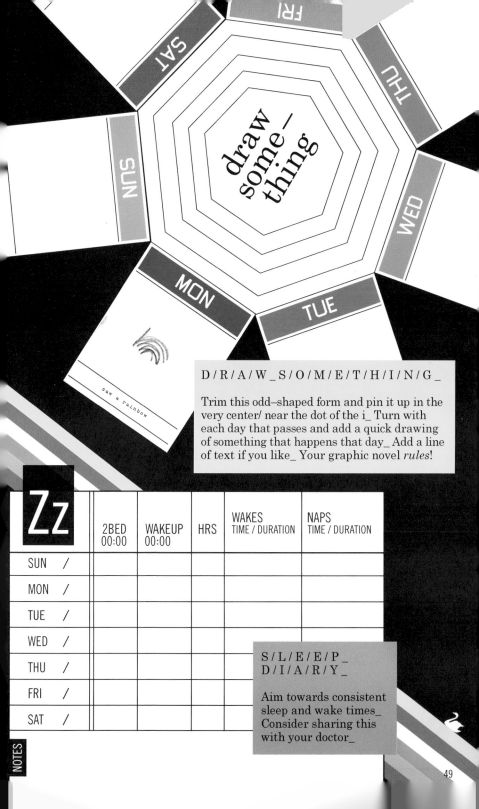

saw a rainbow

D / R / A / W _ S / O / M / E / T / H / I / N / G _

Trim this odd–shaped form and pin it up in the
very center/ near the dot of the i_ Turn with
each day that passes and add a quick drawing
of something that happens that day_ Add a line
of text if you like_ Your graphic novel *rules*!

Zz

	2BED 00:00	WAKEUP 00:00	HRS	WAKES TIME / DURATION	NAPS TIME / DURATION
SUN /					
MON /					
TUE /					
WED /					
THU /					
FRI /					
SAT /					

**S / L / E / E / P _
D / I / A / R / Y _**

Aim towards consistent
sleep and wake times_
Consider sharing this
with your doctor_

NOTES

or you/ll want
y access your
tion updated_

Know the signs_ List the most significant symptoms that indicate you are heading towards or are in a depressive period_ If you are able to catch it early it/ll be easier to manage_ Some find it helpful to distinguish between mild/ moderate and severe signs_ Consider ranking this list_

Choose yo
phone nun
members /
media pal
emotional
this docun
therapist

S / E / C / R / E / T _ F / I / L / E / S

A couple times in this book I talk about time travel_ Are you ready for your ultimate voyage? The formulas are all in these files/ perhaps your most useful tools_ Send the future you reminders of what helps you when you feel depressed_ And/ yeah/ when you/re ready/ I invite you to share this with a few select people_ So maybe the files seem the *opposite* of /secret/ but what makes them so is they will reveal magic mental health healing powers that were secret and unknown/ even to you/ until now_

NOTES

ACTION

area when one of the other
_ Or > add extra requests of
on the unhelpful+repetitive
e when depressed – so you/ll
how very untrue they are –
a powerful quote/ basically
ght help you in the future_

And> action! Begin a list of activities large and small that have positive effects on your mood_ The list will grow as you experiment and discover tools that are uniquely yours_

Get good h
the people
comfort < a
to plan act

do

say

TEAM

the full name and
closest friends / family
neighbors / social
you can count on for
n you/re ready/ share
_ Give a copy to any
you confide in_

_____

_____

_____

_____

_____

_____

_____

_____

HELP

ple actions/words
can use to provide
tivation >_ Ask them
ur < action > list_

_____ don/t do

_____

_____

_____

_____

_____ don/t say

_____

_____

_____

_____

_____

DO IT> I/ve saved the most important list for last_Use this page to note anything that helps you when you/re depressed/ from activities you enjoy to great distractions to meditation to graphic novels to banana splits_ Jot down a fave tv show you could reconnect with_ Add one of your favorite places_ < I have Peter Pan Donuts in Brooklyn in my secret file_ > Add ideas from this book and others you/ve enjoyed_

As the list grows/ share it with select friends or family members/ as many people as you feel comfortable_ The template is available at rainbowsthebook.com but creating a simple Google Drive list works great_

The sad truth is that/ while rationally we know what helps us/ in the moment we most need it we tend to forget what we know helps_ This list is like a note to self but better cuz now your bestie knows what kind of cookies to make you when you feel down_ Win win_ Seriously/ though/ it can be hard to be around people when one is depressed but it/s also hard for them as they don/t know how to help you_ Now they do_

Think about it_ You make this list of things you find helpful and you have built yourself an arsenal_ You share this list with those closest to you and now you have an army_

I kept an ongoing list for 5+ years_ It grew and grew and with it I wrote this book/ and the nine others to follow_

You are gonna do something even cooler_

YOUR NAME HERE

you win!

PAINT
IT
BLACK

if you enjoyed
this book pls leave a
review on Amazon
thank you so much!
i love u/

Buddy

However you feel/ there is a song waiting
to hug it out_ I made a Spotify BLACK
playlist and it features nearly 100 songs with
the word ^black^ in the title_ Maybe your
new theme song is there? Have a listen_
spoti.fi/2qyrbE4

YOU GOT THIS ON LOCK

can you find the
other unbolted
lock?

FOLD IT

E / M / E / R / G / E / N / C / Y
R / E / S / O / U / R / C / E / S

PHONE call 911
1–800–273–TALK (8255)

CRISIS TEXT LINE txt 741741

ONLINE + CHAT
suicidepreventionlifeline.org
spsamerica.org

IN PERSON visit your nearest_
emergency room
urgent care center
walk-in clinic

U / P _ N / E / X / T >
B / L / U / E _

I/m not a doctor – I/m more of the college dropout type – but in the next chapter >> B / L / U / E << I/ll share personal stories and tips about finding professional help/ taking medication and what a stay in a mental hospital might look like_ Also we/ll talk with some actual doctors about >>

- [ ] medication do/s + don/ts
- [ ] individual + group therapy
- [ ] why sleep is so important
- [ ] basic nutrition boosts
- [ ] mindfulness

B / O / N / U / S >> I/ll also share the mood turnaround skill that changed my life AND we/re going skydiving_ See you in the clouds_

Printed in Great Britain
by Amazon